Harold R Foster

Prince Valiant

COMPRISING PAGES 1327 THROUGH 1372

Arn, Son Of Valiant

FANTAGRAPHICS BOOKS

ABOUT THIS EDITION:

Produced in cooperation with the Danish publisher Interpresse and several other publishers around the world, this new edition of *PRINCE VALIANT* is intended to be the definitive compilation of Hal Foster's masterpiece.

Although "Arn, Son Of Valiant" is billed as "Volume 30," this is in fact only the fifth American release in a new series of *PRINCE VALIANT* books. Future releases (Vol. 31 through Vol. 40) are planned to follow sequentially, reprinting the strip until Foster's last work on it in the early '70s. The volumes will be released at the rate of two or three a year, with hopes of eventually graduating to a quarterly schedule.

Additionally, Interpresse and Fantagraphics Books intend to publish the first 25 volumes (comprising Foster's first 22 years on the strip) as an ongoing, "parallel" series, with the ultimate goal of having 40 volumes in print, reprinting the complete *PRINCE VALIANT* by Hal Foster.

ABOUT THE PUBLISHER:

Celebrating its 10th anniversary in 1986, FANTAGRAPHICS BOOKS has dedicated itself to bringing readers the finest in comic book and comic strip material, both new and old. Its "classics" division includes the eight-volume *The Complete E.C. Segar Popeye* and the monthly *NEMO: The Classic Comics Library*. Its "modern" division is responsible for such works as Yellow Kid Award-winner *Love and Rockets* by Los Bros. Hernandez, Peter Bagge's *Neat Stuff*, and the science-fiction color comic *Dalgoda*. See the back cover for a complete listing.

PREVIOUS VOLUMES IN THIS SERIES:

Volume 26: "Lithway's Law"
Volume 27: "The Eternal Quest"
Volume 28: "The Savage Girl"
Volume 29: "Monastery of the Demons"

PRINCE VALIANT, Volume 30
"Arn, Son of Valiant"
comprising pages 1327 (July 15, 1962) through 1372 (Hay 26, 1963)
Published by Fantagraphics Books, 4359 Cornell Road, Agoura, CA 91301
Editorial Co-Ordinator: Henning Kure
Colored by Camillo Conti
Cover inked by Gorm Trasgaard and colored by Søren Håkansson.
Fantagraphics Books staff: Kim Thompson & Tom Mason

Printed in Belgium
ISBN 0-930193-22-9
First printing: Spring, 1987

Prince Valiant
IN THE DAYS OF KING ARTHUR
WRITTEN AND ILLUSTRATED BY HAROLD R FOSTER
Our Story: WITH A FAIR WIND ALETA'S FLEET ROUNDS THE TIP OF BRITTANY AND COMES TO ANCHOR IN A SHELTERED BAY. THEN THE CAPTAINS ARE CALLED TO COUNCIL AND THE GREAT TRADING ADVENTURE BEGINS. FOR SAFETY THEY WILL SAIL IN GROUPS OF THREE, AND THE GOODS OF THE EAST ARE TO BE BARTERED FOR TIN AND FURS, ORNAMENTS OF GOLD, COTTON, AMBER AND AMBERGRIS.

ALL GOES WELL UNTIL BOLTAR IS INFORMED THAT HE IS TO CONVOY TWO MERCHANTMEN TO THULE. "BY THE HAMMER OF THOR!" HE BELLOWS, "BOLTAR, KING OF SEA ROVERS, NURSEMAID TO FOXY HUCKSTERS? NO!"

PRINCE VALIANT AND QUEEN ALETA ARE OF ROYAL BIRTH, AUTOCRATS BOTH, AND TO HAVE THEIR AUTHORITY DENIED IN PUBLIC IS ENOUGH TO JUSTIFY CENSURE.... BUT NOT THE UPROAR THAT FOLLOWS.

"BOLTAR, STOP YOUR BELLOWING, A HERD OF WALRUS MAKES LESS NOISE!" ALETA HAS TO SHOUT TO MAKE HERSELF HEARD. THEN, MORE GENTLY; "YOU WILL NOT HAVE TO BE A NURSEMAID, THIS VESSEL WILL MAKE A THIRD, AND YOU MAY CONDUCT OUR ROYAL FAMILY SAFELY TO CAMELOT."
© King Features Syndicate, Inc., 1962. World rights reserved.
1327.

HAL FOSTER
"SPLENDID WIFE YOU HAVE THERE, VAL. KNOWS BETTER THAN TO GIVE ORDERS TO MEN, WHAT? I WISH MY TILLICUM..." AT THE MENTION OF HIS WIFE'S NAME HE LOOKS OFF INTO THE DISTANCE. BOLTAR, THE LUSTY SEA ROVER, HAS BECOME HOMESICK!
NEXT WEEK- The Voice
7-15-62

Our Story: BOLTAR'S HEART TURNS HOMEWARD, LONGING FOR HIS NATIVE HEATH. BUT FIRST HE MUST LAND PRINCE VALIANT AND HIS FAMILY ON THE SHORES OF BRITAIN.

WITH A FULL COMPLEMENT OF WARRIORS THE DRAGONSHIP MUST REPLENISH ITS SUPPLIES OFTEN. IT IS SUNDAY AND THE MONASTERY BELLS ARE RINGING AS THEY ENTER THE LITTLE PORT.

VAL AND ALETA CLIMB THE HILL AND ARE WELCOMED BY THE ABBOT. THEN THEY HEAR 'THE VOICE' CLEAR AND THRILLING AS A TRUMPET ON A FROSTY MORNING.

THE BROTHERS IN PROCESSION GO TO SERVICE CHANTING, BUT 'THE VOICE' DOMINATES ALL, FILLING THE HALLS AND CORRIDORS WITH ITS MUSICAL SOUND.

"WOJAN HAS FINISHED HIS TRAINING AND WOULD LIKE TO RETURN TO BRITAIN TO FULFILL HIS MISSION, AND THESE TWO SCHOLARS, HIS FRIENDS SLEATH AND DUSTAD, WOULD LIKE TO ACCOMPANY HIM. MAY THEY SAIL WITH YOU?" ASKS THE ABBOT.

VAL AGREES, FOR THERE IS SINCERITY AND SIMPLE HONESTY IN WOJAN'S FACE. THE TWO SCHOLARS MAKE LITTLE IMPRESSION AS THEY STAND HUMBLY BEHIND 'THE VOICE'.

1328.

DURING THE SHORT VOYAGE WOJAN PREACHES AND THE SCHOLARS STAND ON EACH SIDE PROMPTING HIM. THE VIKINGS CANNOT UNDERSTAND HIM BUT HIS RINGING VOICE BRINGS MEMORIES OF ANCIENT HERO SAGAS. AND SO IT IS THAT VAL, IN ALL INNOCENCE, BRINGS TO BRITAIN A FORCE THAT WILL ROCK THE KINGDOM.

NEXT WEEK-**Aruak**

7-22-62

Our Story: THE LONG JOURNEY THAT HAD TAKEN THEM TO DISTANT SEAS AND STRANGE LANDS IS AT AN END. PRINCE VALIANT AND ALETA BID BOLTAR FAREWELL WITH SMILES THAT HIDE THE NEARNESS OF TEARS. FOR IN THESE PERILOUS TIMES EACH FAREWELL MIGHT BE THE LAST.

WOJAN REFUSES TO RIDE AND HUMBLY WALKS THE DUSTY ROAD TO CAMELOT. HIS TWO FRIENDS, SLEATH AND DUSTAD, FREE AT LAST FROM THE RIGORS OF MONASTIC LIFE, ACCEPT ALL THAT IS OFFERED.

BACK IN CAMELOT ONCE MORE, THEIR FAMILIAR ROOMS AND THE NOISE AND BUSTLE OF COURT LIFE SEEM ALL THE MORE EXCITING AFTER THE LONG SEA VOYAGE.

THEN VAL IS SUMMONED BEFORE KING ARTHUR AND MUST TELL OF HIS FAILURE TO ESTABLISH A SAFE ROAD TO ROME. *"ALL EUROPE IS IN TURMOIL AND THE BARBARIANS RAID UP TO THE VERY WALLS OF ROME!"*

THE AUDIENCE OVER, VAL IS FREE TO VISIT THE STABLES, TO SEE HIS WAR HORSE, ARVAK. IN THE COURTYARD WOJAN IS PREACHING, BUT NOW A CROWD OF WORKERS AND SERVANTS HAVE LEFT THEIR WORK TO LISTEN TO HIS VOICE.

ARVAK HAS RETURNED TO HIS WILD STATE. A MAN-KILLER, NO STALL COULD HOLD HIM.

 1329.

IN THE PASTURE ARVAK IS MONARCH, NO STALLION DARE CHALLENGE HIS RULE. MANY OWNERS ARE CLAMORING FOR THEIR MOUNTS, BUT THE HOSTLERS DARE NOT FACE THE GREAT RED STALLION TO GET THEM.

7-29-62 NEXT WEEK- **Oat Cakes**

Our Story: TOO LONG HAS PRINCE VALIANT BEEN AWAY. HIS GREAT WAR HORSE, ARVAK, HAS AGAIN BECOME A MAN-KILLER. HE RULES THE PASTURE AS A MONARCH, AND EVEN THE BOLDEST KNIGHTS COMPLAIN THAT THEY CANNOT GET THEIR RIDING HORSES AWAY FROM HIM.

ARVAK'S LEGS ARE SCARRED FROM KICKING DOWN STALLS AND FENCES; HIS NECK AND SHOULDERS BEAR THE MARKS OF BATTLE WITH OTHER STALLIONS, BUT HE RAISES HIS HEAD AT VAL'S WHISTLE.

OF ALL ANIMALS THE HORSE AND THE DOG TAKE PRIDE IN SERVING MAN, BUT EACH HAS A MEMORY AND ARVAK REMEMBERS THE BRUTALITY OF HIS FIRST MAN......

....AND HOW THAT MAN HAD TRIED TO MAKE HIS WILL SUPREME BY BREAKING THE SPIRIT OF HIS HORSE. AND ON THAT AWFUL DAY HE HAD BROKEN LOOSE AND BECOME A MAN-KILLER.

ARVAK ALSO REMEMBERS HAPPIER DAYS UNDER A NEW MASTER WHEN, IN THE CRASH OF BATTLE, HE HAD GLORIED IN HIS STRENGTH. THERE WAS TRUST AND COMPANIONSHIP TOO IN THE JOUST AS MASTER AND MOUNT BECAME AS ONE.

ARVAK APPROACHES AND LOOKS AT ALETA EXPECTANTLY. IN A FLASH VAL REMEMBERS THE DRUID PRIESTESS. IT WAS A WOMAN WHO HAD FIRST SHOWN THE PROUD HORSE ANY KINDNESS. AND SHE HAD FED HIM OATCAKES!

IF A DRUID PRIESTESS COULD WIN HIS TRUST, WHY NOT ALETA? MEMORIES OF A BITTER PAST MUST BE ERASED, AND TRUST IN HIS MASTER RESTORED.

VAL IS SO INTENT ON REGAINING HIS GREAT WAR HORSE THAT HE DOES NOT NOTICE THAT NOW THE RINGING VOICE OF WOJAN HAS EMPTIED THE KITCHENS, THE STABLES AND THE ARMORY. EVEN THE KNIGHTS AND THEIR LADIES THRONG THE GALLERIES.

NEXT WEEK-**Pride**

1330. 8-5-62

Our Story: KING ARTHUR HAS TRIED TO BRING CHRISTIANITY TO BRITAIN WITH GENTLENESS AND LOGIC BACKED UP WITH THE SWORD. BUT NOW HE IS IN FAIR WAY OF STARVING BECAUSE OF THAT FAITH.

FOR THE KITCHENS, STABLES, ARMORY AND STOREHOUSES ARE EMPTIED AS ALL CROWD AROUND WOJAN TO HEAR HIM PREACH AND LISTEN TO THE THRILLING SOUND OF HIS CLARION VOICE.

VAL IS ABLE TO ENLIST THE HELP OF SEVERAL KNIGHTS, WHO ARE ONLY TOO WILLING TO AID IN THE TAMING OF THE GREAT RED STALLION, SO THEY CAN RECLAIM THEIR OWN HORSES FROM HIS DOMINATION.

THE CORRAL HAS AN ESCAPE WAY WHERE ONLY A MAN CAN SQUEEZE THROUGH, AND THERE STANDS ALETA, AN OATCAKE IN HER OUTSTRETCHED HAND. VAL, IN FULL ARMOR, WHISTLES THE FAMILIAR CALL.

AT THE SIGNAL THE KNIGHTS TROOP BY IN ALL THE PANOPLY OF WAR, LEATHER CREAKING, BITS AND SPURS JINGLING, TRUMPETS SOUNDING.

THE MEMORIES OF A BITTER PAST FADE, FOR THERE BEFORE HIM ARE ALL THE THINGS HE HOLDS MOST DEAR. A GENTLE WOMAN WITH OATCAKES, A COMPANION HE CAN OBEY WITH PRIDE, AND BROTHER WAR HORSES ON PARADE.

ONLY FOR AN INSTANT DOES ARVAK TREMBLE, FOR HE CAN FEEL THE FEAR IN THE HEARTS OF THE STABLE BOYS. BUT CALM, CONFIDENT VOICES REASSURE HIM.

1331.

FROM THAT VALHALLA WHERE ALL WAR HORSES GO, A HUNDRED ANCESTORS LOOK DOWN WITH PRIDE AS THEIR DESCENDANT TAKES HIS RIGHTFUL PLACE AT THE HEAD OF THE TROOP, NECK ARCHED AND HOOFS PRANCING LIKE A DANCER.

NEXT WEEK- **Famine**

8-12-62

Our Story: MANY A MARE STARES BROKEN-HEARTED AFTER ARVAK AS HE GIVES UP HIS OVERLORDSHIP OF THE HERD AND ONCE AGAIN BECOMES A PROUD WAR HORSE, PRANCING AT THE HEAD OF THE TROOP.

AFTER HIS WILD, FREE LIFE AS UNDISPUTED MONARCH OF THE HERD ARVAK IS IN NEED OF MUCH GROOMING. PRINCE VALIANT MUST ATTEND TO THIS HIMSELF, AS THERE ARE NO STABLE BOYS AROUND.

THE CHIEF BUTLER ANNOUNCES THAT DINNER IS DELAYED, FOR COOKS AND SERVANTS HAVE LEFT THEIR WORK TO LISTEN TO THE PREACHING OF WOJAN.

"SIR VALIANT, YOU ARE RESPONSIBLE FOR BRINGING WOJAN TO OUR COURT. TELL ME IF HE IS THE GREAT TEACHER, NAY, THE PROPHET HE IS SAID TO BE, OR A TROUBLE MAKER!"
"I WILL STAKE MY HONOR ON HIS HONESTY," ANSWERS VAL, "BUT I WILL TRY TO FIND OUT MORE ABOUT HIM."

GREAT CROWDS NOW GATHER TO HEAR WOJAN PREACH; SPELL-BOUND THEY LISTEN TO THE RINGING VOICE. THE MAN'S DEEP SINCERITY CARRIES BOTH CONVICTION AND MYSTERY. BUT WHAT DOES HE SAY? TAG ENDS OF SERMONS, QUOTATIONS FROM THE SCRIPTURES, SCRAPS FROM LATIN PRAYERS. ONLY WHEN HIS ADVISORS PROMPT HIM DOES HE MAKE SENSE --

"WE MUST ALL MAKE SACRIFICE, FOR THE WORD MUST GO FORTH TO THE ENDS OF THE EARTH! A CATHEDRAL MUST BE ERECTED AND CHURCHES BUILT AS FORTRESSES AGAINST PAGANISM!"

WOJAN LEAVES WITH THE TWO SCHOLARS, BUT SLEATH HANGS BACK AND, WHEN WOJAN HAS GONE WITHIN, DIRECTS SOME SERVANTS TO GO AMONG THE THRONG AND TAKE UP A COLLECTION FROM THOSE WHO WISH TO MAKE A 'SACRIFICE'.

ALL IS AS IT SHOULD BE; THE EVANGELIST IS NOT CONCERNED WITH MONEY MATTERS BUT LEAVES COLLECTIONS TO HIS ASSISTANTS. YET VAL IS UNEASY. WOJAN HAS THE POWER TO UPSET ALL CAMELOT..... WHAT IF THAT POWER WERE MISUSED?

NEXT WEEK- **The Interview**

1332. 8-19-62

WOJAN AND THE TWO SCHOLARS HAVE QUARTERS ABOVE THE STABLE, AND VAL IS REMINDED OF THE KING'S REQUEST.

SO HE PAYS A VISIT TO WOJAN. IT IS A STRANGE INTERVIEW, FOR THE SCHOLARS, SLEATH AND DUSTAD, GIVE ALL THE ANSWERS. ONE THING VAL LEARNS; THAT WOJAN HAS THE SIMPLE MIND OF A CHILD AND TRUSTS IN THE WISDOM OF HIS TWO ADVISORS.

BUT WHEN VAL MENTIONS THE COLLECTIONS WOJAN IS WROTH. *"COLLECTIONS!"*, HE BELLOWS, *"WHAT COLLECTIONS? OUR ORDER IS PLEDGED TO POVERTY, FOR MONEY IS EVIL."*

"IT IS THE ROOT OF EVIL", ADMITS SLEATH, *"BUT WE MUST FIGHT EVIL WITH EVIL. MANY CONVERTS WILL FOLLOW YOU AND MUST BE FED, YOUR CATHEDRAL BUILT, AND THIS MONEY IS A FREE GIFT!"*

"I WOULD YOU HAD NOT BROUGHT WOJAN TO CAMELOT, SIR VALIANT. KNIGHTS, ARCHERS, SERVANTS AND SERFS NEGLECT THEIR DUTIES TO HEAR HIM PREACH."

HAL FOSTER

RELIEF FROM THESE WORRIES COMES UNEXPECTEDLY. SLEATH AND DUSTAD APPEAR AND REQUEST THE KING FOR HORSES, A WAGON, SUPPLIES AND A CONTRIBUTION.

"OUR MASTER WILL GO FORTH TO PREACH AGAINST EVIL AND CARRY THE WORD TO THE PAGANS AS SOON AS WE ARE EQUIPPED."

THE KING READILY AGREES EVEN THOUGH THE REQUEST SMACKS OF BLACKMAIL.

1335.

NEXT WEEK - **The Exodus**

8-26-62

Our Story: IT IS THE DAY OF WOJAN'S DEPARTURE FROM CAMELOT, AND KING ARTHUR AND PRINCE VALIANT LISTEN TO HIS FAREWELL SERMON, AND THE WORDS, SPOKEN IN HIS COMPELLING VOICE, FILL THEM WITH UNEASINESS.

"THERE IS BUT ONE KING WHOSE LAW YOU MUST OBEY. HE IS THE KING OF KINGS ON HIGH. ALL EARTHLY KINGS ARE DUST AND MUST RETURN TO THE DUST FROM WHICH THEY SPRANG!" POOR SIMPLE WOJAN DOES NOT KNOW HE IS UNDERMINING THE AUTHORITY OF THAT EARTHLY KING, ARTHUR.

THEN WOJAN PASSES THROUGH THE GATES, WALKING BARE FOOT AS USUAL, BUT HIS TWO ADVISORS, THE SCHOLARS SLEATH AND DUSTAD, RIDE THE HORSES THE KING HAS GIVEN THEM.

AT FIRST A FEW ZEALOTS FOLLOW THEIR TEACHER, THEN OTHERS JOIN, AND STILL OTHERS UNTIL A CONTAGION SEIZES ALL CAMELOT. SERVANTS, HOSTLERS, SMITHS AND EVEN GUARDSMEN DROP THEIR TOOLS AND JOIN THE PROCESSION.

VAL AND THE KING LOOK AT EACH OTHER IN AMAZEMENT. THEY HAVE WITNESSED THE BIRTH OF ONE OF THOSE STRANGE RELIGIOUS FERVORS THAT MARK THE DARK AGES, BEGINNING WITH THE QUEST OF THE GRAIL AND ENDING IN THE CRUSADES.

"I HAVE TRIED TO BRING CHRISTIANITY TO OUR REALM WITH LAW AND ORDER, BUT HAVE NOT BEEN ABLE TO RAISE SUCH ENTHUSIASM. HAVE I FAILED?"

1334. 9-2-62

WOJAN'S SIMPLE HEART OVERFLOWS WITH JOY. HE LEADS A GREAT THRONG THAT GROWS LARGER AS PEASANTS LEAVE THEIR FIELDS TO JOIN THE RANKS. THERE IS NO DISCIPLINE AND ALL ARE GROWING HUNGRY.

NEXT WEEK- **The Growing Menace**

Our Story: BECAUSE PRINCE VALIANT IS ONE OF THE VERY FEW WHO CAN READ BOOKS, HAS TRAVELED WIDELY, AND WAS A PUPIL OF WISE MERLIN, HE STANDS HIGH IN KING ARTHUR'S COUNCIL.

"WHAT OF THIS WOJAN, SIR VALIANT? HE GATHERS A MULTITUDE TO HEAR HIM PREACH, AND THEREAFTER THEY DENY OUR AUTHORITY. DOES HE PREACH SEDITION?"

"NO, SIRE, HE IS HONEST AND CHILDLIKE, BUT HE TRUSTS HIS ADVISERS BECAUSE OF THEIR SUPERIOR LEARNING, AND THEY MAY PROMPT HIM TO SAY THINGS THAT HAVE A DOUBLE MEANING."

IT IS EVEN AS VAL SAYS. SLEATH AND DUSTAD ARE NOW WEALTHY WITH THE GIFTS AND CONTRIBUTIONS THAT POUR IN (AND WHICH THEY KEEP), AND LOOK DOWN ON WOJAN AS A TOOL TO THEIR PLANS. AND WOJAN, SO ELATED AT THE SUCCESS OF HIS CRUSADE, FAILS TO NOTICE THIS.

WOJAN'S COMPELLING VOICE THRILLS HIS LISTENERS AND HIS JUMBLED SERMONS ONLY CREATE MYSTERY. PEASANTS AND SERFS LEAVE HOME AND FIELD TO JOIN THE AIMLESS PILGRIMAGE, FOR IT IS RUMORED THAT THE MASTER WILL LEAD THEM TO ETERNAL BLISS.

BUT HUNGER KNOWS NO MORALITY AND, UNKNOWN TO WOJAN, THE PILGRIMS PLUNDER AND LAY WASTE TO THE LANDS OVER WHICH THEY WANDER.

THE KING HEARS OF THE GROWING MENACE. *"THIS WOJAN HAS SUCH A HOLD ON THE IMAGINATION OF THE ZEALOTS WHO FOLLOW HIM THAT TO CURB HIM MIGHT START THAT MOST TERRIBLE OF THINGS, A HOLY WAR. AND WITH US ON THE WRONG SIDE!"*
"SIRE," SAYS VAL QUIETLY, *"I THINK I HAVE A SOLUTION!"*

NEXT WEEK - **The Humble Abbot**

1335. 9-9-62

Our Story : PRINCE VALIANT ARISES AND ADDRESSES THE KING: "SIRE, THIS WOJAN IS REGARDED AS A SAINT BY HIS MULTITUDE OF FOLLOWERS. TO CURB HIM BY FORCE WOULD START A TERRIBLE HOLY WAR. YET HE MUST BE STOPPED, FOR WHEREEVER HIS AIMLESS PILGRIMAGE WANDERS THE LAND IS LAID WASTE."

"MY LADY ALETA AND I VISITED A MONASTERY IN BRITTANY," VAL CONTINUES. "THE ABBOT WAS A HUMBLE, KINDLY MAN, AND HIS AUTHORITY OVER THE BROTHERS WAS GREAT."

"IT WAS HE WHO ASKED ME TO BRING WOJAN TO BRITAIN. THE HABIT OF OBEDIENCE IS HARD TO BREAK. WOJAN MAY ACCEPT THE COUNSEL AND ADVICE OF HIS ABBOT."

AND SO IT IS THAT VAL BRINGS THE ABBOT OUT OF BRITTANY AND THEY FOLLOW THE TRAIL OF RUIN THAT MARKS THE PASSAGE OF THE PILGRIMS.

THEY ENTER A VILLAGE UNTOUCHED BY THE THIEVES AND BULLIES THAT FOLLOW ON THE FRINGE OF THE PILGRIMAGE FOR THE SAKE OF PLUNDER.

"WE PAID FOR OUR SAFETY," THE MAYOR SAYS. "DUSTAD AND SLEATH OFFERED TO LEAD THEIR FOLLOWERS AWAY FROM OUR VILLAGE. THE PRICE WAS HIGH, BUT WE HAD HEARD WHAT HAPPENED TO OTHER VILLAGES, SO WE PAID."

THE OLD ABBOT SHAKES HIS HEAD. SUCH VILLAINY HE CAN HARDLY IMAGINE.

NEXT WEEK–**Tribute**

1336. 9-16-62

Prince Valiant
IN THE DAYS OF KING ARTHUR
WRITTEN AND ILLUSTRATED BY HAROLD R FOSTER
Our Story: AS PRINCE VALIANT AND THE ABBOT DRAW EVER CLOSER TO THE PILGRIM HOST THE FULL HORROR OF THEIR PASSING UNFOLDS. THE OLD, THE LAME AND THE SICK ARE LEFT BEHIND TO DIE IN A PLUNDERED LAND.

HUNGER AND SUFFERING CREATE FANATICS; FOOD CAN RESTORE REASON. VAL SENDS A MESSAGE TO THE KING REQUESTING A WAGON TRAIN OF PROVISIONS.

WOJAN KNOWS NOTHING OF THE MENACE HE HAS CREATED, FOR SLEATH AND DUSTAD SURROUND HIM WITH A WELL-FED GUARD. THEIR WEALTH IS MOUNTING AND SOON, WITH A MAN REGARDED AS A SAINT TO DO THEIR BIDDING, THEY WILL BE THE STRONGEST FORCE IN BRITAIN.

THE NEXT VILLAGE VAL AND THE ABBOT COME TO IS BEING PILLAGED AND BURNED IN WANTON DESTRUCTION. ITS PEOPLE HUDDLE IN THE CHURCH FOR PROTECTION.

THE HALF-NAKED RABBLE ARE NO MATCH FOR AN ARMORED KNIGHT WITH A FLASHING SWORD AND MOUNTED ON A GREAT RED WAR HORSE WHOSE FLAILING HOOFS SCATTER THEM IN FEAR.
© King Features Syndicate, Inc., 1962. World rights reserved.

HAL FOSTER
AGAIN THE NAMES OF SLEATH AND DUSTAD COME UP. "WE PAID THEM A GREAT SUM FOR PROTECTION, BUT WE HAVE BEEN BETRAYED."
NEXT WEEK-The Reckoning
1337.
9-23-62

Our Story: PRINCE VALIANT AND THE ABBOT HAVE SEEN MISERY, VIOLENCE AND BETRAYAL IN THE WAKE OF THE PILGRIM HORDE. NOW THE ODOR OF AN UNWASHED MULTITUDE BECOMES STRONGER AND, DESPITE THE DISCOMFORT, THE ABBOT URGES HIS MOUNT INTO A GALLOP.

A VAST CROWD SURROUNDS A KNOLL UPON WHICH WOJAN STANDS, AND HIS GLORIOUS VOICE HOLDS THEM SPELLBOUND AND SILENT. ALTHOUGH THEY ARE TOO FAR AWAY TO UNDERSTAND HIS WORDS, THERE CAN BE NO DOUBT OF HIS DEEP SINCERITY.

VAL AND THE ABBOT DISMOUNT AND MAKE THEIR WAY THROUGH THE HUNGRY RABBLE AND ENTER WOJAN'S PAVILION.

THIS IS THE GREAT TEST. WILL THE ABBOT STILL HOLD ANY AUTHORITY OVER HIS OLD PUPILS?
WOJAN RISES AND HUMBLY KNEELS TO RECEIVE THE ABBOT'S BLESSING.

"MY SON, YOU HAVE DONE NOBLY," SAYS THE ABBOT KINDLY, *"BUT NOW IT IS TIME TO BUILD YOUR CATHEDRAL WITH THE TREASURE YOU AND YOUR ADVISERS HAVE GATHERED."*

"TREASURE!" ECHO'S WOJAN IN ASTONISHMENT. *"WHAT TREASURE?"*

1338

HAL FOSTER

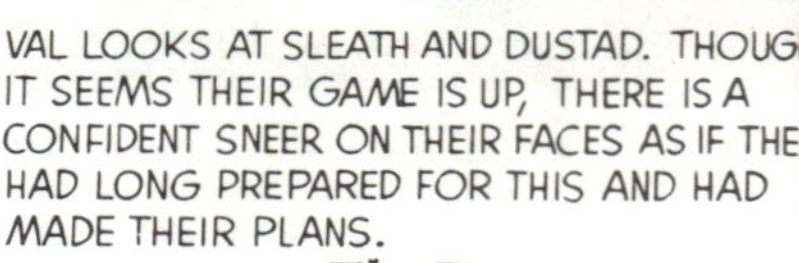

VAL LOOKS AT SLEATH AND DUSTAD. THOUGH IT SEEMS THEIR GAME IS UP, THERE IS A CONFIDENT SNEER ON THEIR FACES AS IF THEY HAD LONG PREPARED FOR THIS AND HAD MADE THEIR PLANS.

NEXT WEEK - **The Treasure.**

9-30-62

Our Story: PRINCE VALIANT AND THE ABBOT AT LAST CATCH UP WITH THE VAST HORDE OF PILGRIMS, AND THE CRUEL HOAX IS REVEALED. WOJAN IS STUNNED.

"YOU, MY LEARNED AND RESPECTED FRIENDS, YOU HAVE USED OUR HOLY MISSION TO MAKE A PROFIT?" EXCLAIMS WOJAN, LOATH TO BELIEVE SUCH GREED

"YES, YOU STUPID FOOL," SNARLS SLEATH, "WE ARE NOW MEN OF GREAT WEALTH AND POWER, AND YOU WILL DO AS WE DIRECT!"

"YOU ARE BUT A CHILD WITH A VOICE. IT IS WE WHO PUT THE WORDS IN YOUR MOUTH. WE MADE YOU AND WE CAN BREAK YOU!"

SLEATH AND DUSTAD ARE SO USED TO TREATING WOJAN AS AN INNOCENT CHILD THAT THEY HAVE FORGOTTEN THAT HE IS ALSO A MAN, A STRONG AND ANGRY MAN.

"GUARDS! GUARDS!" SHRIEKS THE BATTERED SLEATH, AND THE GROUP OF WELL-FED AND PAID BULLIES THEY HAD ASSEMBLED TO KEEP WOJAN FROM LEARNING THE TRUE STATE OF AFFAIRS, COME RUNNING.

"GUARD THE WAGONS! BELLOWS DUSTAD.

"THAT MUST BE WHERE THE TREASURE IS HIDDEN. COME, WOJAN, AND TRULY EARN THE PRICE OF YOUR CHURCH. AND A THOROUGHLY AROUSED WOJAN FOLLOWS VAL TO THE WAGONS.

NEXT WEEK- **The Fight for the Treasure**

1339.

10-7-62

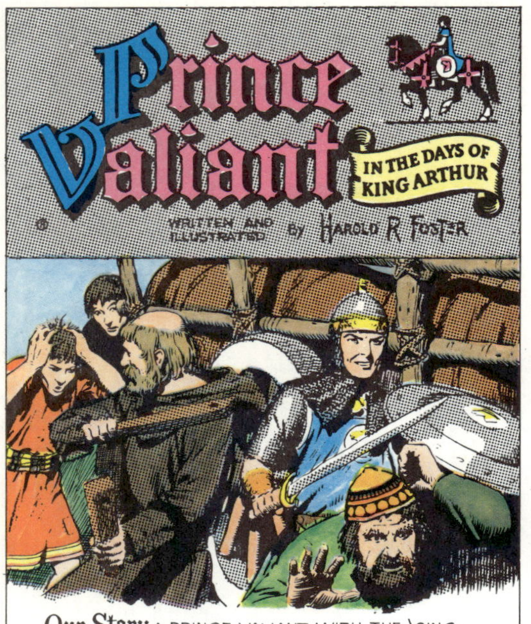

Our Story: PRINCE VALIANT WITH THE 'SINGING SWORD' STANDS BACK TO BACK WITH WOJAN AND HIS CUDGEL, AND VERY FEW OF THE HIRED BULLIES ARE BRAVE ENOUGH TO DO BATTLE. THE REST SWARM OVER THE WAGONS, CLAWING AT THE TREASURE CHESTS.

NOT UNTIL THEY MOUNT THE WAGONS DOES THE REAL BATTLE BEGIN, AND IT IS FIERCE, FOR GREED IS SOMETIMES A SUBSTITUTE FOR COURAGE.

THE STARVING PILGRIMS BECOME AWARE THAT THEIR BELOVED PROPHET IS BEING ATTACKED AND VIOLENCE SWEEPS THE MULTITUDE LIKE A GRASS FIRE. IN THE TUMULT NO ONE KNOWS WHO HIS FOE IS.

CLEAR AS A BUGLE NOTE ON A BATTLEFIELD THE VOICE OF WOJAN RINGS OUT. BUT NOW VAL IS HIS PROMPTER. *"PEACE! PEACE!"* HE CALLS, *"FOR OUR LONG SUFFERING IS OVER. BY THE GRACE OF OUR GOOD KING ARTHUR, FOOD FOR ALL IS ON ITS WAY!"*

IT IS THE ABBOT HIMSELF WHO TENDS TO WOJAN'S WOUNDS. *"FEAR NOT, MY SON, GOOD WILL YET COME FROM ALL THIS EVIL. EVEN NOW MY CLERK IS COUNTING THE TREASURE, AND YOUR CHURCH MAY BE BUILT."*

1340.

FAR INTO THE NIGHT THE DELIGHTED ABBOT WORKS ON PLANS FOR THE CHURCH. BUT AS HIS CLERK COUNTS THE TREASURE, THE PROJECT GETS BIGGER; A CLOISTER IS ADDED, A MONASTERY, GARDENS, A HOSPITAL......

ONLY VAL IS UNEASY. DID HIS MESSAGE REACH THE KING? DID THE KING RESPOND? HOW LONG CAN THIS STARVING RABBLE BE HELD IN CHECK?

NEXT WEEK- **The Reward**

10-14-62

Our Story: WOJAN AND THE ABBOT LISTEN HAPPILY AS THE CLERK COUNTS THE TREASURE. SLEATH AND DUSTAD HAVE BEEN VERY ENTERPRISING CROOKS AND THE TREASURE IS GREAT. ONLY PRINCE VALIANT IS WORRIED. WILL THE KING SEND FOOD FOR THE STARVING PILGRIMS..... AND WHAT TO DO WITH THE TWO RASCALS?

THE CLERK SOLVES THE LAST PROBLEM. *"I WAS A MAN OF DUBIOUS MORALS, WISE IN THE WAYS OF THE WORLD, BEFORE I JOINED THE BROTHERHOOD. I CAN SOLVE THE PROBLEM OF SLEATH AND DUSTAD WITHOUT BOTHERING THE KING."*

THE TWO SCOUNDRELS ARE AWAITING THE KING'S JUSTICE; THE CERTAINTY THAT THEY WILL SOON DECORATE THE GALLOWS HAS SERIOUSLY INTERFERED WITH THEIR PLANS FOR A LIFE OF EASE.

"YOU, SLEATH AND DUSTAD, ARE FREE TO GO," SAYS THE WILY CLERK. *"THOUGH YOUR METHODS WERE DISHONEST YOU HAVE MADE WOJAN'S CHURCH AND MONASTERY POSSIBLE. HERE IS YOUR REWARD. NOW GO!"*

WITH GREEDY EYES THEY EXAMINE THEIR REWARD: TWO WINE CUPS OF SOLID GOLD INLAID WITH AMETHYST. THEY ALSO BECOME AWARE OF OTHER GREEDY EYES. THEIR RUFFIAN BODYGUARD HAS GATHERED AROUND THEM.

THE PRECIOUS GOBLETS MIGHT HAVE MADE SLEATH AND DUSTAD COMFORTABLY RICH, BUT, AS THEY WERE NEVER HEARD OF AGAIN, WHO KNOWS?

HAL FOSTER

THE CLERK RETURNS WITH GOOD NEWS. *"A MESSAGE HAS COME SAYING THAT A WAGON TRAIN OF PROVISIONS IS BUT A LEAGUE AWAY, AND"*... WITH A PIOUS SMIRK: *"I REWARDED OUR TWO BENEFACTORS. THEY ARE GREEDY MEN AND, ALAS, ARE FOLLOWED BY OTHER GREEDY MEN."*

NEXT WEEK- **Succor**

1341.

10-21-62

1342.

HAL FOSTER

ALETA SHOULD BE CONTENT, FOR COURT LIFE IN CAMELOT IS BRIGHT AND GAY, HER FAMILY LOUD AND HEALTHY. BUT SHE IS LONELY. WHY BE MARRIED TO A GREAT BIG GORGEOUS HERO IF HE IS NOT AT ONE'S SIDE? SHE PLANS A PILGRIMAGE OF HER OWN.

NEXT WEEK - **Romance**

10-28-62

Our Story: CAMELOT IS A GAY PLACE, BUT WITHOUT HER PRINCE VALIANT AT HER SIDE ALETA IS LONELY. SHE DREAMS OF THEIR GLORIOUS, ROMANTIC PAST; OF THE TIME SHE CAUSED A MINOR EXPLOSION BY USING THE SORCERY THAT SEEMS TO COME NATURALLY TO SMALL BLONDES WITH GREY EYES.

SHE HAD WAVED THOSE INCREDIBLY LONG LASHES UP AT HIM AND EARNED SOME CRUSHED RIBS AND A WHOLLY SATISFACTORY DECLARATION........

.....AND THAT TIME WHEN SHE HAD OVERDONE THE IMPUDENCE, AND HE HAD TOSSED HER INTO THE FISH POND! SUCH A MAN! WHAT A MAGNIFICENT BRUTE!

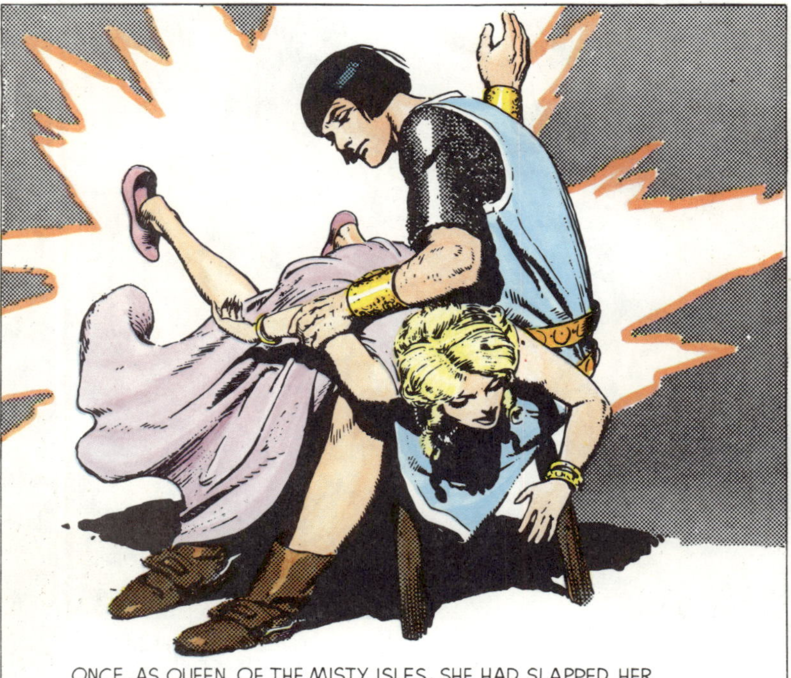

ONCE, AS QUEEN OF THE MISTY ISLES, SHE HAD SLAPPED HER FAVORITE SUBJECT. THAT WAS THE TIME HE HAD POINTED OUT SHARPLY THAT SHE WAS ALSO A WIFE. OH! ONE COULDN'T HELP LOVING SUCH A GORGEOUS CREATURE!

HE HAD BEEN GOOD TO HER IN OTHER WAYS TOO. JUST SO SHE WOULD NOT BE LONELY WHEN HE WENT ADVENTURING, HE HAD SURROUNDED HER WITH FOUR ACTIVE CHILDREN, THE DEAR.

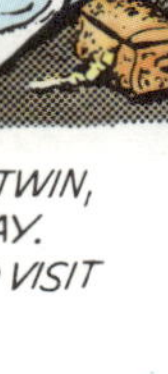

ALETA EXPLODES INTO ACTION; *"KATWIN, MIND THE CHILDREN WHILE I AM AWAY. ARN, GET READY TO RIDE, WE GO TO VISIT YOUR FATHER!"*

1343.

ALETA IS A QUEEN, REPORTED TO BE QUITE PRETTY AND, THEREFORE, POSSESSED OF A LARGE AMOUNT OF VANITY. WHEN SHE HAS PACKED WHAT SHE CONSIDERS THE BARE NECESSITIES, IT TAKES MANY BAGGAGE ANIMALS TO CARRY THE LOAD.

NEXT WEEK- **The Safari**

11-4-62

Our Story: ALETA WEARIES OF COURT LIFE AND LONGS TO BE WITH PRINCE VALIANT ONCE MORE. HIS ABSENCE HAS MADE HER HEART GROW FONDER (NOT LOGICAL OF COURSE, BUT FEMININE). SHE TAKES ARN ALONG TO GIVE HIM EXPERIENCE.

BUT ARN HAS TRAVELED ALL THE WAY TO BAGDAD WITH HIS FATHER AND HAS LEARNED MUCH. IT IS HE WHO CHOOSES THE CAMPING PLACE WITH AN EYE TO WATER, GRAZING AND DEFENSE, POSTING SENTRIES AND SENDING OUT SCOUTS.

THE SCOUTS BRING BACK FRIGHTENING STORIES; SOME OF THE STARVING PILGRIMS LEARNED FIRST TO FORAGE FOR FOOD, THEN TO PILLAGE, AND FINALLY TO BECOME DANGEROUS GANGS OF ROBBERS.

ONLY BECAUSE THEY ARE WELL MOUNTED DID THEY ESCAPE CONTACT WITH SOME OF THESE GANGS. AT LAST A SCOUT TELLS THEM THAT THE NEXT DAY WILL SEE THE END OF THEIR JOURNEY. ALETA PREPARES FOR THE MEETING WITH ALL THE SKILL AT HER COMMAND.

THE MEETING IS FAR FROM ROMANTIC. VAL IS DOWN IN A MUDDY HOLE DIRECTING THE WORKERS, AND THERE IS LITTLE RESEMBLANCE TO A WARRIOR PRINCE.

"OH, HUSBAND, YOU ARE SO BEAUTIFULLY DIRTY, SO HANDSOMELY SMUDGED!" SHE EXCLAIMS, *"AND YOU HAVE PUT ON SO MUCH WEIGHT..... ALL MUD!"*

NEXT WEEK- **To Save the Treasure**

11-11-62

Our Story: ALETA TIRES OF COURT LIFE AND MAKES A LONG JOURNEY TO BE ONCE MORE WITH PRINCE VALIANT. AND VAL HAS BEEN TOILING ON THE NEW CHURCH WITH SUCH ARDOR THAT HE HAS FORGOTTEN ABOUT HIS APPEARANCE.

ALETA'S PAVILION IS PUT UP ON A PLEASANT STREAMSIDE GROVE, AND VAL COLLECTS HIS BELONGINGS FROM THE LEAKY TENT HE HAS SHARED WITH WOJAN AND THE ABBOT.

FOR A BRIEF MOMENT VAL LOOKS BACK TO WHERE HE HAS LIVED THE SIMPLE LIFE, SLEEPING UNDER HIS CLOAK ON A BED OF DAMP RUSHES. WITH A SIGH HE TURNS TOWARD ALETA'S LUXURIOUS PAVILION.

ALETA SINGS GAILY AS SHE UNPACKS HER DAINTY THINGS, AND SOON THE TENT TAKES ON THE APPEARANCE OF AN ORIENTAL BAZAAR AND SMELLS LIKE A FLOWER GARDEN.

ALETA HAS NO HANDMAIDEN TO KEEP THINGS IN ORDER, AND VAL WATCHES HIS ARMS AND ARMOR DISAPPEAR UNDER A CLOUD OF BRIGHT SCARVES AND GOWNS. SOON NO ONE CAN FIND ANYTHING.

IN THE MUD-AND-WATTLE VILLAGE WHERE THE WORKERS ARE QUARTERED VAL FINDS TWO YOUNG WOMEN TO ACT AS MAIDS, AND HE IS FREE TO CONTINUE WORK ON THE CHURCH.

 1345.

ONE DAY VAL AND ARN ARE STANDING HIGH ON THE SCAFFOLD AND VAL POINTS EASTWARD. *"THERE, WHERE THE MISTS HANG LOW, ARE THE FENS WHERE I SPENT MY BOYHOOD, A WILD AND BEAUTIFUL PLACE FULL OF MYSTERY AND ADVENTURE."* ARN IS SILENT AS HE GAZES INTO THE DISTANCE - MYSTERY! ADVENTURE!

11-18-62

NEXT WEEK - **Memories of the Past.**

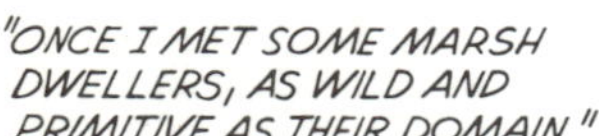

"I SHOWED THEIR BOY HOW TO SPEAR THE GREAT PIKE."

"AND HE IN TURN TAUGHT ME TO SNARE WILDFOWL WITH A WEIGHTED NET. AS THE YEARS WENT BY I HAD MANY ADVENTURES. ONCE THE MUD RELEASED THE BONES OF A HUGE CREATURE THAT DWELT IN THE MARSH IN OLDEN TIMES."

ARN IS INTERESTED AND ASKS A THOUSAND QUESTIONS, AND IT IS FAR INTO THE NIGHT BEFORE HE IS SATISFIED.

Our Story: WHEN PRINCE VALIANT REALIZES THAT THE STREAM BY WHICH THEY ARE CAMPED RUNS INTO THE FENS, HE REGALES HIS SON ARN WITH STORIES OF THE ADVENTUROUS BOYHOOD HE SPENT THERE. ARN DOES NOT DELAY. NEXT DAY HE IS ON HIS WAY TO SEEK HIS OWN ADVENTURES.

TOWARD EVENING ARN DISCOVERS THE FENS ARE REALLY A MYSTERIOUS PLACE. THERE ARE DOZENS OF CHANNELS, LAKES, PONDS, WATER-MEADOWS. LOST! HE WONDERS IF HIS FATHER EVER FELT THE TOUCH OF FEAR HE NOW FEELS.

1348.

HE TURNS AROUND AND RETRACES HIS ROUTE. NIGHT FINDS ARN RIGHT BACK WHERE HE STARTED.

12-9-62

Prince Valiant
IN THE DAYS OF KING ARTHUR
WRITTEN AND ILLUSTRATED BY HAROLD R FOSTER

Our Story: AT DAWN OF THE FIFTH DAY ARN STARTS OUT ONCE MORE TO FIND A WAY OUT OF THE VAST SWAMPLANDS.

PRINCE VALIANT, IN A BORROWED DUGOUT, IS ALSO ON HIS WAY. ARN MUST LEARN TO LOOK AFTER HIMSELF, BUT PERHAPS HE IS NOT READY FOR SUCH A TEST AS THIS.

THE FENS HAVE CHANGED; SOME LAKES ARE CHOKED WITH WEEDS, CHANNELS HAVE CHANGED THEIR COURSE. VAL MARKS HIS PASSAGE.

OUTCASTS AND FUGITIVES LURK HERE. WELL HE REMEMBERS HIS MEETING WITH THORG AND WONDERS IF THE MONSTER STILL LIVES HERE.

FATHER AND SON SLEEP TEN MILES APART, AND VAL SLEEPS UNCONCERNED, FOR HE HAS FORGOTTEN HOW SCARY THE FENS CAN BE FOR A SMALL BOY.

OCCASIONALLY HE SENDS A BUGLE NOTE ACROSS THE MARSH AND LISTENS FOR AN ANSWERING CALL.

 1349.

HAL FOSTER
AT LAST VAL MEETS ARN. HE IS PEERING DOWN INTO THE WATER TO READ IN THE SWAYING WEEDS THE DIRECTION OF THE CURRENT. AND THERE, CROUCHING ABOVE HIM, IS THE SINISTER GRAY FORM OF THORG. NEXT WEEK-The Gift

12 - 16 - 62

IT HAS BEEN WHETTED DOWN TO A FRAGILE THINNESS. VAL TOSSES HIM HIS OWN SAXEKNIFE, AND IT IS RECEIVED WITH A JOYFUL WHIMPER. VAL SIGNALS TO ARN AND THEY PADDLE AWAY, LEAVING THE WILD CREATURE TO GLOAT OVER HIS TREASURE.

VAL SPENT HIS BOYHOOD HUNTING HERE. THE CALL OF THE WIDE MARSHES IS TOO MUCH TO BE IGNORED, SO HE AND ARN GO HUNTING TOGETHER.

THE YOUNG DUCKS ARE JUST BEGINNING TO FLY, AND DECOY READILY. TIME FLIES BY UNNOTICED.

1350

HAL FOSTER

THE HUNTERS RETURN TRIUMPHANT, FORGETTING ALL THEIR ADVENTURES IN THE PRIDE OF THEIR SKILL. BUT ALETA REMEMBERS A WEEK OF FEARFUL ANXIETY. *"YOU HEARTLESS BRUTES,"* SHE WAILS. VAL SHAKES HIS PUZZLED HEAD. THEY ARE BACK SAFELY. WHAT WAS THERE TO WORRY ABOUT? OH, THESE WOMEN!

NEXT WEEK-**Ethwald the businessman**

12-23-62

Our Story: PRINCE VALIANT TAKES ALETA IN HIS ARMS. IT IS AN OLD REMEDY FOR TEARS. BUT HE WONDERS WHY SHE SHOULD WORRY SO WHEN HE AND ARN ARE IN DANGER. DOESN'T SHE TRUST THEM?

NOW IT IS TIME TO RETURN TO DUTY AT CAMELOT, AND WOJAN AND THE ABBOT ASK HIM TO CARRY OUT AN IMPORTANT MISSION.

"WHEN YOU LEAVE, SIR VALIANT, OUR TREASURE WILL NO LONGER BE SAFE," THE ABBOT EXPLAINS. *"WE WISH YOU WOULD TAKE IT TO CAMELOT WITH YOU."*

"REMNANTS OF THE PILGRIM HOST HAVE FORMED INTO LARGE BANDS AND STILL PILLAGE THE COUNTRYSIDE."

PROOF OF THIS IS NOT LONG IN COMING. SOME TRAVELERS HAVE A BRUSH WITH THESE OUTLAWS AND TAKE REFUGE IN THE HALF-FINISHED MONASTERY.

UNTIL THE KING SENDS A TROOP TO DISPERSE THESE RUFFIANS, THE LAND ROUTE TO CAMELOT WILL BE PERILOUS. VAL RIDES TO THE COAST AND CHARTERS A SHIP SO THEY CAN GO BY SEA.

WHEN HE RETURNS, THE TRAVELERS BEG TO TAKE PASSAGE WITH HIM AS FAR AS THEIR FIEF ON THE COAST NEAR HASTINGS.

1351

VAL IS MORE INTENT ON THE PROPER CARE OF ARVAK THAN THE STOWAGE OF THE TREASURE. NOT SO HIS GUESTS......

12-30-62

.....THEIR LEADER, ETHWALD, RAISES HIS EYEBROWS AT THE SIGHT OF THE CHESTS. THEREAFTER HE SPENDS HIS TIME PLANNING FOR AN OPULENT FUTURE.

NEXT WEEK- **The Quarry**

Our Story: A FAIR WIND BLOWS AND THE VOYAGE TO CAMELOT BEGINS. THE SHIP IS CROWDED WITH THE GUARD FOR THE TREASURE CHESTS, THE HORSES, PRINCE VALIANT, HIS FAMILY AND THE GUESTS.

ETHWALD PROVES TO BE A VERY ENTERTAINING GUEST AND REGALES THEM WITH TALES OF HUNTING ADVENTURES IN THE WEALD, THAT GREAT FOREST REGION NEAR HIS FIEF

THE SHIP IS WALLOWING UP THE CHANNEL WHEN THE WATER CASKS SPRING A MYSTERIOUS LEAK. *"I KNOW A SHELTERED COVE WHERE THE CASKS CAN BE FILLED FROM A SPARKLING BROOK,"* OFFERS ETHWALD.

IT IS JUST AS HE SAID, AND THE CASKS ARE TOWED ASHORE TO BE FILLED. ETHWALD AND HIS FRIENDS PROPOSE A FEW HOURS OF HUNTING TO PASS THE TIME AWAY, AND INVITE ARN TO JOIN THEM.

THE PARTY REACHES THE TOP OF THE DOWNS AND SEES THE GREAT FOREST OF THE WEALD STRETCHING INTO THE DISTANCE. *"LOOK, THERE IS A STRONGHOLD ON YONDER HILL,"* SAYS ARN, POINTING. *"WHOSE IS IT?"*
"MINE," ANSWERS ETHWALD SLYLY, AND, AT HIS SIGNAL, ARN IS SEIZED.

THE CASKS HAVE BEEN FILLED AND STOWED LONG SINCE. THE DAY IS ENDING, AND YET NO SIGN OF THE HUNTING PARTY. VAL AND ALETA ARE WORRIED.

 1352.

A SKIFF PUTS OUT FROM SHORE; A NOTE IS DELIVERED AND THE BOATMAN PULLS AWAY IN THE DARKNESS. A RANSOM NOTE!

1-6-63

AND ARN, LOCKED IN A DUSTY ROOM, WONDERS IF HE WILL EVER BE ABLE TO TRUST ANYONE ANY MORE.

NEXT WEEK- **Cough Medicine**

Our Story: PRINCE VALIANT READS THE LETTER DEMANDING RANSOM FOR HIS SON ARN. THEN HE GATHERS ALL AVAILABLE FIGHTING MEN AND, IN A TOWERING RAGE, GOES TO FIND SIEUR ETHWALD'S STRONGHOLD.

ETHWALD GREETS THEM CHEERFULLY. *"GOOD DAY, SIR VALIANT. AS YOU VERY WELL KNOW YOU HAVE NOT SUFFICIENT MEN TO STORM THESE WALLS, BUT IF YOU WILL LEAVE YOUR ARMS OUTSIDE, YOU MAY ENTER IN SAFETY TO DISCUSS A MATTER OF BUSINESS."*

"YOUR SON, PRINCE ARN, IS A FINE LAD. YOU MUST BE VERY PROUD OF HIM. HE IS WELL WORTH THE TREASURE CHESTS YOU HAVE ABOARD YOUR SHIP." AND ETHWALD LAUGHS PLEASANTLY AND ORDERS REFRESHMENTS.

VAL RETURNS TO THE SHIP. *"PAY THE RANSOM AND GET ARN BACK,"* ADVISES ALETA, *"THEN LAY SIEGE BEFORE THE WALLS UNTIL WE CAN SUMMON HELP FROM THE KING."* VAL SHAKES HIS HEAD, *"THE TREASURE IS IN MY SAFEKEEPING AND IS NOT MINE TO GIVE."*

"WELL, THE LEAST YOU CAN DO IS SEND ARN THE MEDICINE FOR HIS COLD," ALETA SNAPS, *"EVEN IF HE DOES COMPLAIN IT TASTES LIKE POISON."*

1353.

AS HE WATCHES ALETA BUSY WITH HER MEDICINE CHEST AN IDEA IS FORMING IN HIS MIND.

1-13-63

AND SOON THEY ARE CONCOCTING A BITTER BUT ALMOST HARMLESS POTION THEY HOPE WILL CURE ETHWALD OF HIS GREED.

NEXT WEEK-**Sleight-of-Hand**

Our Story: PRINCE VALIANT CLIMBS THE CLIFF TO ETHWALD'S STRONGHOLD TO ARRANGE RANSOM FOR THE RETURN OF HIS SON, ARN, AND HE CARRIES A VIAL OF NAUSEATING CHEMICALS UNDER HIS GREAT CAPE.

WHEN HE STATES HIS MISSION HE IS ADMITTED AND STANDS BEFORE THE TRIUMPHANT ETHWALD.

"THE CLIMB UP THE CLIFF HAS MADE ME THIRSTY," SAYS VAL. HIS HOST ORDERS WINE TO BE SERVED. HE IS IN A JOVIAL MOOD, FOR WILL HE NOT SOON BE RICH?

UNDER COVER OF HIS CLOAK VAL EMPTIES THE VIAL INTO HIS HALF-EMPTY GOBLET.

"ON YONDER KNOLL RANSOM AND HOSTAGE WILL BE EXCHANGED," AND VAL DRAWS ETHWALD'S ATTENTION AWAY LONG ENOUGH FOR HIM TO SWITCH THE GOBLETS.

"MUCH AS I ABHOR CRIME I MUST DRINK TO YOUR CLEVERNESS." THEN VAL DRAINS HIS GLASS.

1354

ETHWALD DOES LIKEWISE. A PUZZLED LOOK CROSSES HIS FACE, HIS MOUTH TWISTS IN A GRIMACE; HE GAZES WITH STARING EYES AT THE CRYSTALS ON THE BOTTOM OF HIS GOBLET. *"POISON!"* HE CRIES.

1-20-63

"YES," ANSWERS VAL PLEASANTLY, *"YOU HAVE TWO VERY UNPLEASANT DAYS TO LIVE, BUT QUEEN ALETA, WHO IS SKILLED IN CHEMISTRY, MIGHT GIVE YOU AN ANTIDOTE. AT A PRICE, OF COURSE."*

NEXT WEEK- **The Cure**

Our Story: "*I HAVE BEEN POISONED!*" CROAKS ETHWALD HOARSELY. "*GUARDS, SEIZE PRINCE VALIANT.*" THEN TURNING TO VAL HE WHEEZES, "*YOU AND YOUR SON WILL DIE UNLESS THE ANTIDOTE AND THE TREASURE ARE SENT TO ME AT ONCE.*"

"*YOU KNOW HOW THESE CLEVER WOMEN ARE,*" ANSWERS VAL CHEERFULLY. "*THEY ARE NOT TO BE TRUSTED.*"

"*THE QUEEN HAS A TERRIBLE TEMPER,*" LIES VAL. "*DO NOT ANGER HER, SHE MIGHT SAIL AWAY WITH BOTH THE ANTIDOTE AND THE TREASURE. SHALL WE GO TO HER AT ONCE?*"

"*VERY WELL, BUT I WILL HOLD YOUR SON, ARN, AS HOSTAGE FOR MY SAFE RETURN.*"

VAL IS QUITE SYMPATHETIC. "*OH, ETHWALD, DO NOT TEMPT FATE. ALREADY THE POISON IS EATING AWAY YOUR ENTRAILS AND IT IS NO TIME TO QUIBBLE.*"

"*IF YOU DO NOT RETURN HER SON, THE QUEEN WILL BE WROTH AND WILL MOST LIKELY GIVE YOU A MORE POWERFUL POISON INSTEAD OF THE ANTIDOTE.*" AND ETHWALD, NOW IN THE GRIP OF FEAR, HAS ARN RELEASED.

HE PLEADS WITH ALETA FOR AN IMMEDIATE CURE, BUT, BEING A WOMAN, SHE HAS QUITE A LOT TO SAY ABOUT DELINQUENT KNIGHTS, AND NOTHING CAN STOP HER.

"*WHAT WAS THE 'POISON' YOU GAVE HIM?*" ASKS VAL. ALETA GIGGLES: "*MUSTARD, ALUM AND BITTER ROOT.*"

"*NO WONDER HE THOUGHT HIMSELF POISONED,*" SAYS VAL. "*AND WHAT WILL YOUR SO-CALLED ANTIDOTE CONSIST OF?*"

"*RANCID FISH OIL, WORMWOOD, HONEY AND GALL,*" ANSWERS ALETA SWEETLY, "*TO BE TAKEN EVERY HOUR.*"

NEXT WEEK - **The Hero**

1555. 1-27-63

Our Story: ETHWALD IS CONVINCED THAT HE HAS BEEN POISONED, AND WITH GOOD REASON; FOR THE POTION ALETA HAD CONCOCTED FOR HIM WILL GUARANTEE HIM CRAMPS FOR SOME TIME.

BUT SHE HAS GRACIOUSLY CONSENTED TO MIX AN ANTIDOTE, WHICH IS WORSE. RANCID FISH OIL, SALT, GALL, MUSTARD AND HONEY ARE AMONG THE INGREDIENTS. AFTER A GENEROUS DOSE OF THIS 'CURE' HE LEAVES THE CABIN...

....WHILE LEANING OVER THE RAIL ETHWALD DISCOVERS THAT THE SHIP'S BOATS ARE TOWING THE VESSEL OUT OF THE COVE TO THE OPEN SEA.

HE ACCUSES ALETA OF TREACHERY! NOW, THIS IS THE WRONG THING TO SAY TO A MOTHER WHOSE SON HE HAS HELD FOR RANSOM. PRINCE VALIANT, A MARRIED MAN OF SOME EXPERIENCE, MAKES AN EFFORT TO SAVE HIM, BUT TOO LATE!

AN HOUR PASSES DURING WHICH POOR ETHWALD LEARNS ALL ABOUT THE FLAWS IN HIS CHARACTER AND MANY MORE HE DID NOT EVEN SUSPECT. HE ALSO LEARNS THAT HE IS BEING TAKEN TO CAMELOT AND THE KING'S JUSTICE.

ONCE AGAIN PRINCE VALIANT RETURNS TO CAMELOT A HERO, A QUEST WELL DONE. THE AWFUL PILGRIMAGE IS OVER, THE TREASURE FOR THE ABBEY DELIVERED SAFELY

1356.

NOW ALETA HAS WORK TO DO. THIS SMUG AND POMPOUS HERO MUST BE REDUCED TO THE MODEST, ATTENTIVE HUSBAND SHE LOVES SO WELL.

NEXT WEEK-**War Clouds**

2-3-63

Our Story: FOR TWO MONTHS NOW WAR CLOUDS HAVE SHADOWED THE NORTH COUNTRY, YET KING ARTHUR SEEMINGLY DOES NOTHING. BUT NOW THE TIME HAS COME ONCE AGAIN TO SECURE THE REALM, AND HIS IMPATIENT KNIGHTS ARE EAGER FOR THE FRAY.

PROMOTION COMES TO A YOUNG PAGE. ARN IS SUMMONED BEFORE SIR BALDWIN AND INFORMED THAT HE IS NOW A NOVICE AND MAY TRAIN FOR COMBAT.

YOUNG NOBLES MUST SERVE AS PAGE BOYS TO LEARN COURTLY MANNERS, BUT ARN HAS BEEN TAUGHT COURTESY SINCE CHILDHOOD. IT IS DOUBTFUL IF ANY OTHER PAGE HAS RECEIVED BETTER INSTRUCTION IN OBEDIENCE, RESPECT AND CHIVALRY THAN HE .....

.....NOR DOES ANY NOVICE HAVE A BETTER OR MORE SEVERE TEACHER. OVER AND OVER HE SPEEDS DOWN THE COURSE WITH LANCE OR SWORD UNTIL HORSE AND RIDER BECOME AS ONE.

THEN SIR BALDWIN SEES HIM PERFORM AND AGAIN PROMOTES HIM, THIS TIME TO BACHELOR. ARN IS THE YOUNGEST OF THIS GROUP AND TAKES MANY A BEATING.

THE WEARY, PAINFUL DAYS DRAG BY, THE LUMPS AND BRUISES MULTIPLY, BUT AT LAST HE GETS THE REWARD HE HAS BEEN HOPING FOR: *"YOU ARE DOING FAIRLY WELL. WE MAY MAKE A WARRIOR OF YOU YET,"* HIS SIRE ADMITS.

THE WAR COUNCIL HAS COMPLETED THEIR PLANS, AND THE CAPTAINS ARE CALLED IN TO BE ASSIGNED THEIR DUTIES. AND THEY NOTE WITH SATISFACTION THE SUBTLE CHANGE IN THEIR KING. THIS IS ARTHUR, LEADER OF MEN, THE MOST FEARED WARRIOR IN ALL BRITAIN!

NEXT WEEK- **The Foe**

2-10-63

Prince Valiant
IN THE DAYS OF KING ARTHUR
WRITTEN AND ILLUSTRATED BY HAROLD R FOSTER
Our Story: THE KING OF NORTH WALES DIES, AND HIS SON CIDWIC MOUNTS THE THRONE. AT ONCE HE SUMMONS HIS VASSAL NOBLES, EACH TO BRING A LEVY OF SOLDIERS ON A WAR FOOTING. ONCE NORTH WALES EXTENDED NORTHWARD INTO SCOTLAND, AND IT HAS LONG BEEN HIS AMBITION TO REGAIN THE LOST TERRITORY AND, PERHAPS, ADD MORE.

WITH SOUNDING TRUMPETS AND WAVING BANNERS CIDWIC BEGINS HIS MARCH. ONLY ONE MAJOR OBSTACLE STANDS IN HIS WAY; THE WALLED CITY OF CARLISLE, BUILT LONG AGO BY THE ROMANS TO GUARD THE WESTERN END OF HADRIAN'S WALL

IF CIDWIC TAKES CARLISLE, HE CAN, WITH THE PROMISE OF PLUNDER, ENLIST THE WARBANDS OF THE WILD PICTS AND CALEDONIANS AND CONQUER ALL NORTH BRITAIN.
KING ARTHUR ORDERS A FLEET OF SHIPS WITH SUPPLIES AND VETERAN ARCHERS TO THE BELEAGUERED CITY.

BUT THE ONLY ARMY HE SENDS AGAINST CIDWIC IS A TROOP OF LIGHT CAVALRY, ENGINEERS, MASONS AND BUILDERS UNDER THE COMMAND OF SIR KAY

1358.

HAL FOSTER
TO HIS WARRIORS, EAGER FOR ACTION, HE SAYS: "*THE SOLDIERS CIDWIC HAS CALLED UP ARE BOUND TO SERVE ONLY FOR THREE MONTHS, THEN THEY MAY RETURN TO THEIR HOMES TO GATHER THEIR HARVEST. WE WILL RIDE WHEN THE HARVEST MOON IS AT THE FULL.*"
NEXT WEEK- Sir Kay's Task
2-17-63

Our Story: THE ONLY FORCE KING ARTHUR SENDS AGAINST THE AMBITIOUS CIDWIC IS A TROOP OF CAVALRY AND A SMALL ARMY OF WORKMEN UNDER THE COMMAND OF HIS FOSTER-BROTHER, SIR KAY.

AND NOW THE CAVALRY RIDES FORTH, STRIKING AT SUPPLY LINES, COMMUNICATIONS AND FORAGING PARTIES.

CIDWIC HEARS OF THESE RAIDS AND IS PLEASED. IF THAT IS ALL KING ARTHUR CAN SEND AGAINST HIM, HE HAS NOTHING TO FEAR. EVEN IF HE LOSES HIS STRONGHOLD, THE CAPTURE OF CARLISLE AND ITS RICHES WILL GIVE HIM ALL THE STRENGTH HE NEEDS.

BUT CARLISLE DOES NOT FALL. SUPPLIED BY SEA WITH FOOD AND TROOPS, IT RESISTS HIS SIEGE.

 1359.

THE KING SUMMONS PRINCE VALIANT. *"ONLY THE HOPE OF PLUNDER HOLDS CIDWIC'S ARMY BEFORE CARLISLE, BUT AUTUMN IS NEAR AND THEY GROW IMPATIENT TO RETURN TO THEIR HOMES. SELECT A TROOP OF FAST YOUNG RIDERS FROM AMONG THE SQUIRES AND BACHELORS TO ACT AS MESSENGERS, AND KEEP ME INFORMED. TELL SIR KAY OUR ARMY WILL MARCH WITHIN THE WEEK."*

NEXT WEEK - **The Chosen**

2-24-63

1360.

AND THAT MESSENGER IS ARN.

3-3-63

Our Story: FATHER AND SON RIDE IN OPPOSITE DIRECTIONS; ARN TO WARN KING ARTHUR OF CIDWIC'S UNEXPECTED RETREAT FROM CARLISLE.....

....AND PRINCE VALIANT RIDES FURIOUSLY TO HELP SIR KAY DEFEND THE EARTHWORK THAT LIES BETWEEN CIDWIC'S ONRUSHING ARMY AND HIS MOUNTAIN STRONGHOLD.

PRINCE ARN, HIS MESSAGE DELIVERED, DOES NOT LINGER IN THE SAFETY OF THE ADVANCING ARMY, BUT TURNS HIS HORSE AND RACES BACK FOR FURTHER DUTY.

VAL ARRIVES IN TIME. CIDWIC'S STRONGHOLD STANDS BROODING UPON ITS HILLTOP, AND ACROSS THE ROAD SIR KAY'S PALISADE GUARDS THE APPROACHES. IN THE FAR DISTANCE A CLOUD OF DUST GIVES EVIDENCE OF AN APPROACHING ARMY.

SIR KAY IS WARNED IN TIME, THE PALISADES ARE MANNED, AND THE GATE IS CLOSED AS CIDWIC'S ARMY ENCIRCLES THEM LIKE A LIVING TIDE.

BUT NOT BEFORE ONE LONE RIDER ON A SPENT HORSE LIMPS UP TO THE GATE... ...ARN REPORTS FOR DUTY!

1361.

HOPING TO CATCH THE DEFENDERS UNPREPARED, CIDWIC ORDERS AN IMMEDIATE ATTACK IN FORCE. FOR WELL HE KNOWS THAT KING ARTHUR'S KNIGHTS ARE WITHIN THREE DAYS' MARCH.

THE FIRST ATTACK FAILS. A HALT IS CALLED, WHILE SCALING LADDERS AND RAMS ARE MADE AND FIRE-ARROWS PREPARED.

NEXT WEEK- **The Lone Archer**

3-10-63

Our Story: BALKED IN HIS GREAT DREAM OF CONQUEST, CIDWIC IS PREPARED TO TAKE VENGEANCE ON THIS SMALL FORT, AND HE HIMSELF MUST DO HEROIC DEEDS TO REGAIN THE CONFIDENCE OF HIS WARRIORS.

FIRST COMES A RAIN OF FIRE-ARROWS AGAINST THE WOODEN PALISADE AND BUILDINGS. THE FLAMES ARE KEPT UNDER CONTROL UNTIL THE WELL GOES DRY.

RAMS BATTER AT THE GATES AND SOON THE THUNDER OF THEIR BLOWS IS ACCOMPANIED BY THE SPLINTERING OF WOOD.

HEEDLESS OF THEIR LOSSES THEY CROSS THE DITCH WITH SCALING LADDERS AND STORM THE WALLS IN GREAT NUMBERS.

THE HORSES, DRIVEN MAD BY THE FLAMING ARROWS, ARE RELEASED AS THE GATES COME DOWN, AND CRASH THEIR WAY TO FREEDOM OVER THE CRUSHED AND BROKEN BODIES OF THE ENEMY.

THE EXULTANT VOICE OF THE 'SINGING SWORD' CAN BE HEARD AS PRINCE VALIANT DEFENDS THE STAIRWAY, AND WARRIORS FALL LIKE AUTUMN LEAVES BEFORE HIM.

AND FOR GOOD REASON--AN ARCHER IN THE FLAMING TOWER IS MAKING SURE THE ODDS AGAINST HIS SIRE ARE NOT TOO GREAT.

1362.

SO HEAVY ARE THE LOSSES THAT THE ATTACK FALTERS. CIDWIC DRAWS HIS GREAT SWORD. NOW IS THE TIME TO LEAD HIS WARRIORS TO VICTORY!

NEXT WEEK- **The Duel**

3-17-63

 1363.

HAL FOSTER

IN THE LURID GLARE OF THE FLAMING TOWER THE TWO LEADERS FACE EACH OTHER. THE SHOUTING AND CLASH OF ARMS DIE DOWN. *"I HAVE EVER WISHED TO TEST MY SKILL AGAINST A CELEBRATED CHAMPION,"* SAYS CIDWIC.
"I WILL DO MY BEST TO MAKE THE TEST INTERESTING," ANSWERS VAL.

NEXT WEEK - **The Test**

3-24-63

Our Story: AND SO THE EPIC DUEL BEGINS: PRINCE VALIANT, WEARY, BLEEDING AND GASPING FOR BREATH AFTER HOURS OF COMBAT, FACES KING CIDWIC. AND THE YOUNG KING, FRESH AND CONFIDENT, EXHIBITS HIS SKILL.

VAL, CONSERVING HIS STRENGTH, FIGHTS ON THE DEFENSIVE, WHILE CIDWIC, MASTER OF MANY TRICKS, LEAPS TO THE ATTACK; THEN LEAPS BACK, TRYING TO DRAW VAL INTO SOME MISTAKE. VAL STUDIES HIS NIMBLE FOE, SEEKING TO FIND SOME WEAKNESS. OTHER EYES ARE BUSY, TOO.

HAL FOSTER

"HIS RIGHT LEG, SIRE, WATCH HIS RIGHT LEG!" IT IS ARN'S VOICE SPEAKING IN GREEK, HIS MOTHER'S TONGUE, THAT NONE MAY UNDERSTAND HIS WORDS.

TIME AND AGAIN CIDWIC HAS LEAPED BACK TURNING TO THE LEFT, EXPOSING HIS RIGHT LEG BUT PREPARED FOR A COUNTER-STROKE THAT WOULD SEVER VAL'S ARM DID HE STRIKE AT IT. NOW VAL DOES STRIKE. WHEN NEXT CIDWIC MAKES HIS MOVE VAL LEAPS IN, AND HIS SLASHING STROKE FALLS BEFORE CIDWIC CAN RAISE HIS WEAPON FOR THE COUNTER. HE FEELS THE BURNING SHOCK, TRIES TO REGAIN HIS BALANCE, BUT HIS LEG BUCKLES BENEATH HIM AND HE TOPPLES FROM THE GALLERY TO THE COURTYARD BELOW.

NEXT WEEK-**The Spoilsport**

1364.

3-31-63

Our Story: PRINCE VALIANT WATCHES HIS ADVERSARY CRASH TO THE COURTYARD BELOW WITHOUT ANY FEELING OF JOY AT HIS VICTORY. HE IS NUMB WITH FATIGUE.

CIDWIC IS MILDLY SURPRISED AS HE LIES THERE GAZING AT THE BRIGHT SKY. HE FEELS NO PAIN, ONLY A GREAT WEARINESS. THEN HE CLOSES HIS EYES AND PEACE COMES AT LAST TO THE TURBULENT SPIRIT OF CIDWIC, YOUNG KING OF NORTH WALES.

THE MOMENTARY STILLNESS IS SHATTERED BY A YOUNG VOICE SHOUTING THE BATTLE CRY, *"ONWARD! VICTORY! ARTHUR! ARTHUR! ARTHUR!"*

THE ENEMY HAD VICTORY WITHIN THEIR GRASP, BUT NOW, WITH THEIR LEADER GONE, THEY HAVE NOTHING TO FIGHT FOR AND ARE DRIVEN FROM THE OUTPOST.

A CLOUD OF DUST AND THE THUNDER OF HOOFS HERALDS THE ARRIVAL OF KING ARTHUR AND HIS KNIGHTS. THEY HAVE RIDDEN ALL NIGHT TO SURPRISE CIDWIC'S ARMY, BUT THAT ARMY IS SCATTERING IN ALL DIRECTIONS, INTENT ONLY ON REACHING THEIR HOMES.

A VERY YOUNG ARCHER MAY BE FORGIVEN A MOMENT OF PRIDE: *"THE GREATEST OF WARRIORS, NONE MAY EQUAL HIM IN SKILL OR HARDIHOOD, AND HE IS MY SIRE! AND I, PRINCE ARN, HAVE FOUGHT BY HIS SIDE!"*

"WHY DO I ALWAYS HAVE THE MISFORTUNE TO PICK YOU FOR THESE MISSIONS?" GRUMBLES KING ARTHUR, THOUGH THERE IS A TWINKLE IN HIS EYE. *"OUR KNIGHTS HAVE TRAINED HARD AND LONG FOR THIS BATTLE; WE HAVE RIDDEN ALL NIGHT ONLY TO FIND YOU HAVE HAD ALL THE FUN. I AM SORRY TO SAY THIS, SIR VALIANT, BUT YOU ARE A SPOILSPORT!"*

1365.

NEXT WEEK- **Long live the King**

4-7-63

Our Story: THE BODY OF KING CIDWIC IS CARRIED UP TO THE GATES OF HIS STRONGHOLD AND A HERALD ANNOUNCES: *"KING ARTHUR HAS DECLARED A TRUCE FOR TWENTY-FOUR HOURS SO YOU MAY CARE FOR YOUR WOUNDED AND BURY THE DEAD."*

WITH THEIR LEADER KILLED AND THE ARMY SCATTERED, THE STRONGHOLD WISELY SURRENDERS, AND KING ARTHUR ENTERS IN TRIUMPH.

EVEN DEFEAT CANNOT HALT THE RULE OF SUCCESSION, AND CUDDOCK, TWELVE-YEAR-OLD SON OF CIDWIC, IS CROWNED KING OF NORTH WALES.

THEN THE NEW KING IS FORGOTTEN IN THE SERIOUS BUSINESS OF TREATY MAKING.
HE IS BEFRIENDED BY ONE OF THE VETERANS OF THE LATE WAR, AND A FRIENDSHIP DEVELOPS.

KING ARTHUR IS TRYING TO SOLVE THE KNOTTY PROBLEM OF FINDING A REGENT AND SECURING THE FIDELITY OF NORTH WALES, WHEN HE SEES THE TWO BOYS RIDING OUT TOGETHER FOR A DAY OF SPORT.

1366.

"HOLD," HE SAYS, *"MAYBE THAT FRIENDSHIP WILL PROVE A STRONGER BOND THAN AN OATH OF FEALTY SWORN UNDER THE THREAT OF FORCE."*

4-14-63

RUDDAH IS THE YOUNGER BROTHER OF CIDWIC AND, WITH THE DEATH OF THAT KING, HE IS ONE STEP NEARER THE THRONE. NOW ONLY THE BOY KING, CUDDOCK, STANDS IN HIS WAY TO THE POWER HE HUNGERS FOR.

NEXT WEEK- **The Stolen Arrows**

Our Story: TWO BOYS RETURN HOME FROM A DAY OF HUNTING. ONE, PRINCE ARN, THE OTHER THE NEWLY-CROWNED KING OF NORTH WALES. BUT TITLES ARE FORGOTTEN. FORGOTTEN ALSO IS THAT ONLY YESTERDAY THEY WERE ENEMIES.

TOO BAD THAT THIS HAPPY YOUNG KING MUST DIE. BUT THEN HE STANDS IN THE WAY OF HIS UNCLE RUDDAH, WHOSE INSANE DESIRE FOR POWER WILL JUSTIFY ANY CRIME.

THE SIGHT OF ARN'S QUIVER GIVES HIM A PRICELESS IDEA. FOR ARN HAS ALWAYS HAD A KEEN INTEREST IN HUNTING, AND HIS ARROWS ARE DISTINCTIVE, STRAIGHT AND TRUE WITH A RED COCK-FEATHER AND A BLUE BAND.

NOW RUDDAH, SUBTLE AS AN ADDER, PUTS HIS PLAN TO ACTION. *"YOU LADS SEEM TO LIKE A WOMAN'S SPORT, ONE IN WHICH THE HAWKS DO ALL THE WORK. MUCH LIKE THE STUPID DEER HUNTERS WHOSE STAG HOUNDS FIND THE HART AND BRING IT TO BAY SO THAT IT CAN EASILY BE SLAIN."*

"ONLY THE REAL SPORTSMAN HUNTS THE LOWLY RABBIT. FOR THAT TAKES CRAFT, THE SILENT STALK, THE PATIENT WAITING AND THE TRUE FLIGHT OF THE ARROW. DOWN IN THAT HOLLOW IS A WARREN WHERE I TEST MY SKILL. BUT THEN IT IS NO SPORT FOR UNTRAINED BOYS."

NATURALLY THE BOYS ACCEPT HIS CHALLENGE. IN THE MORNING THEY WILL DEMONSTRATE THEIR SKILL ON RABBITS!

RUDDAH SPREADS SUSPICION: *"I DO NOT TRUST THIS ARN. HIS FATHER AND THE FATHER OF THE YOUNG KING WERE ENEMIES AND FOUGHT EACH OTHER. AND ARN MAY SEEK VENGEANCE ON THE KING."*

1367.

AT DAWN RUDDAH, ARMED WITH ARN'S ARROWS, AWAITS THE COMING OF THE TWO LADS.
NEXT WEEK-**When to kick a King**

4-21-63

Prince Valiant
IN THE DAYS OF KING ARTHUR
WRITTEN AND ILLUSTRATED By HAROLD R FOSTER
Our Story: THE RABBIT WARREN IS JUST WHERE RUDDAH HAD TOLD THEM. CIRCLING DOWN WIND THEY APPROACH CAUTIOUSLY THROUGH DENSE BRUSH.

RUDDAH LEAVES HIS LOOKOUT AND STALKS HIS PREY. THAT HE IS ABOUT TO MURDER HIS NEPHEW, WHO IS ALSO HIS KING, DOES NOT BOTHER HIM IN THE LEAST, SO GREAT IS HIS DESIRE FOR POWER.

ARN NOCKS AN ARROW IN READINESS AND MOTIONS CUDDOCK TO SILENCE..... A SILENCE BROKEN BY THE SNAPPING OF A TWIG BEHIND THEM.

ARN TURNS SLOWLY BUT STILL IN TIME TO SEE A HAND HOLDING A BOW AND AN ARROW BEING DRAWN TO THE FULL.

HE LEAPS BACK AND AT THE SAME TIME DELIVERS A SWIFT KICK TO THE YOUNG KING. AN ARROW THUDS INTO A TREE WHERE CUDDOCK WAS STANDING JUST A MOMENT BEFORE!

THERE COMES THE SOUND OF THEIR ASSAIL-ANT CRASHING AWAY THROUGH THE BRUSH, AND ARN SENDS AN ARROW WHISTLING TOWARD THE SOUND.
© King Features Syndicate, Inc., 1963. World rights reserved.
1368.

"LOOK, ARN, ISN'T THAT ONE OF YOUR ARROWS?" AND CUDDOCK POINTS TO THE SHAFT STILL QUIVERING IN THE TREE TRUNK. ARN COUNTS HIS ARROWS.
4-28-63

HAL FOSTER
"SOMEONE HAS STOLEN MY ARROWS. THREE ARE STILL MISSING. FIND WHO HAS THOSE ARROWS, AND WE WILL FIND THE ASSASSIN!"
NEXT WEEK- The Accusing Arrows

Our Story: ONE OF ARN'S MISSING ARROWS STILL QUIVERS IN THE TREE WHERE, A MOMENT BEFORE, THE YOUNG KING CUDDOCK WAS STANDING. *"HAD THAT ARROW FOUND ITS MARK, I WOULD HAVE BEEN ACCUSED OF YOUR MURDER,"* SAYS ARN.

CAUTIOUSLY THE TWO BOYS LEAVE THE WOODS, EXPECTING FURTHER ATTACK BY THE UNSEEN ASSASSIN.

BUT THE ASSASSIN HAS TROUBLES OF HIS OWN. THE ARROW ARN SHOT BLINDLY AT THE MOVEMENT IN THE THICKET PROTRUDES FROM RUDDAH'S SIDE. HE REACHES FOR THE SHAFT AND, TO HIS HORROR, IT MOVES EASILY IN HIS FINGERS.

FOR THE HEAD OF A HUNTING ARROW IS FAST TO THE SHAFT AND CAN BE WITHDRAWN, BUT A WAR ARROW IS TIPPED WITH A BOLT THAT STAYS IN THE WOUND. THERE IS BUT ONE THING TO DO. RUDDAH BACKS AGAINST A ROCK AND PUSHES THE ARROW THROUGH, REMOVES THE BOLT, AND WITHDRAWS THE SHAFT.

"YOUR LIFE IS NOT SAFE UNTIL THE ASSASSIN IS FOUND!" EXCLAIMS ARN. *"I WILL SEEK COUNCIL WITH MY FATHER."*
"AND I WILL GO TO MY UNCLE RUDDAH AND SEEK HIS AID," ANSWERS CUDDOCK.

"THE ASSAILANT STILL HAS YOUR MISSING ARROWS," SAYS VAL. *"THEY WILL PROVE HIS GUILT."*

"MY UNCLE RUDDAH HAD A HUNTING ACCIDENT AND LIES WOUNDED, BUT...." AND THE YOUNG KING HESITATES, *"I FOUND ARROWS OF YOURS IN HIS QUIVER."*

1369.

THE EVIDENCE IS ENOUGH TO CALL A MEETING OF THE COURT. THREE KNIGHTS ARE SENT TO BRING RUDDAH TO STAND TRIAL.

NEXT WEEK- **The Hunt.**

5-5-63

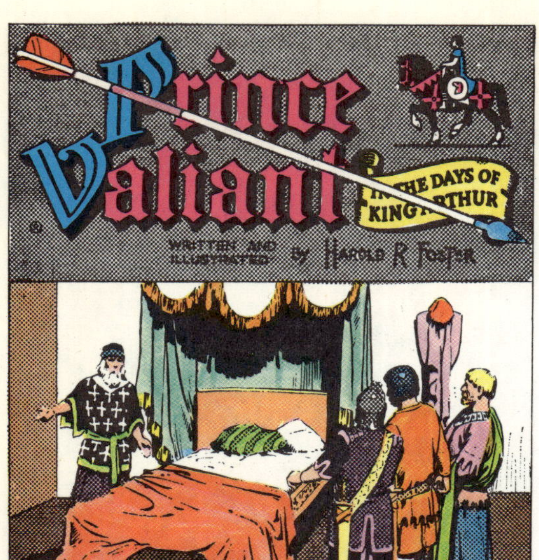

Our Story: THREE KNIGHTS ARE SENT TO BRING RUDDAH TO TRIAL FOR THE ATTEMPTED ASSASSINATION OF THE YOUNG KING. BUT THE GUILTY ONE HAS FLOWN, AND THE COURT PHYSICIAN EXPLAINS: *"I WAS CALLED TO DRESS HIS WOUND, BUT HE HAS DISAPPEARED!"*

HIS OWN CLEVERNESS IS HIS UNDOING. RUDDAH USED PRINCE ARN'S ARROWS IN HIS ATTEMPT TO KILL THE KING, AND NOW POSSESSION OF THOSE ARROWS WILL CONVICT HIM. THE ARROWS MUST BE DESTROYED!

HE STAGGERS TO THE SPORT-HALL BUT FINDS HIS QUIVER EMPTY. THOSE CURSED ARROWS WITH THE RED COCK FEATHER AND THE BLUE BAND, THAT WERE TO PUT THE BLAME ON ARN, ARE GONE!

HE WHO PLOTS AGAINST A KING IS DOOMED TO A VERY UNPLEASANT DEATH. RUDDAH TAKES HORSE AND FLEES.

THERE IS BUT ONE COURSE OPEN TO RUDDAH, TO GATHER A BAND OF DISCONTENTED NOBLES AND REVOLT. HE MUST BE BROUGHT TO TRIAL IMMEDIATELY.

"I DEMAND THIS MISSION," CRIES ARN STOUTLY, "FOR HAD RUDDAH ACHIEVED HIS PURPOSE, IT IS MY HONOR THAT WOULD HAVE BEEN FOREVER QUESTIONED!"

1370.

SO FIRM IS HE IN HIS RESOLVE THAT HE IS GRANTED TWO MEN-AT-ARMS AND GIVEN THE KING'S WARRANT.

5-12-63

HAL FOSTER

HE AND HIS MEN RIDE IN A WIDE CIRCLE, QUESTIONING THE PEASANTS UNTIL THEY FIND ONE WHO SAW RUDDAH PASS...... ON A ROAD THAT LEADS TO THE SEA.

NEXT WEEK-**Haunted Arrows.**

Our Story: PRINCE ARN WITH TWO WARRIORS STARTS OUT IN PURSUIT OF RUDDAH, THAT RUTHLESS ASSASSIN WHO TRIED TO WIN A CROWN BY MURDERING HIS OWN KIN AND PLACING THE BLAME ON ARN.

DAY IS ENDING AND RUDDAH MUST REST, FOR THE WOUND IN HIS SIDE IS THROBBING AND SHOULD BE CLEANSED AND DRESSED.

FROM FAR UP THE VALLEY ARN SEES HIS QUARRY DISMOUNT. UNAWARE OF PURSUIT RUDDAH PREPARES TO REST.

"MY BOW WILL NOT SEND AN ARROW THAT FAR, BUT SEE IF YOUR HEAVIER WEAPON WILL LAND A SHAFT NEAR HIM," SAYS ARN.

RUDDAH IS AROUSED BY THE THUD OF AN ARROW. HE STARES AT IT WILDLY; RED COCK FEATHER AND BLUE BAND! THOSE ACCURSED ARROWS ARE BEGINNING TO HAUNT HIM; A SYMBOL OF HIS GUILT AND DOOM.

WEARILY HE MOUNTS HIS TIRED HORSE AND LETS IT STUMBLE THROUGH THE NIGHT.

1371.

HAL FOSTER

ARN AND HIS MEN RESUME THE CHASE AT THE FIRST HINT OF DAWN. THEY DO NOT KNOW HOW SERIOUS IS HIS WOUND, BUT THEY DO KNOW HIS PROWESS AS A SWORDSMAN. HE WILL BE GIVEN NO REST UNTIL EXHAUSTED

NEXT WEEK-**Down to the Sea.**

5 · 19 · 63

Our Story: FOR THE FIRST TIME IN HIS YOUNG LIFE PRINCE ARN KNOWS HATE. THE FUGITIVE, RUDDAH, IS ALL THAT HE HAS BEEN TAUGHT TO DESPISE; RUTHLESS, CRUEL, TREACHEROUS, AND HE WOULD HAVE SACRIFICED ARN TO HIS AMBITIONS.

ALL DAY THEY HAVE KEPT THEIR WEARY QUARRY IN SIGHT, AND WHEN DARKNESS FALLS ARN CREEPS DOWN TO THE CLUMP OF TREES WHERE HE WAS LAST SEEN.

AS RUDDAH AWAKENS FROM A FITFUL SLEEP THE FIRST THING HE SEES IS AN ARROW WITH BLUE BAND AND RED COCK FEATHER. HALF IN RAGE, HALF IN PANIC, HE CRUSHES THE HAUNTING SYMBOL UNDER HIS HEEL.

EVEN HIS PANIC CANNOT SPEED THE WEARY MOUNT. HE COMES TO A RIVER; A RIVER RUNS TO THE SEA, AT THE SEA THERE MUST BE BOATS, AND ESCAPE!

FROM A HILLTOP ARN LOOKS DOWN UPON THE SPARKLING SEA. ON THE SAND WHERE THE RIVER MEETS THE SEA A BOAT IS DRAWN UP, AND TOWARD THAT BOAT RUDDAH IS MAKING HIS WAY.

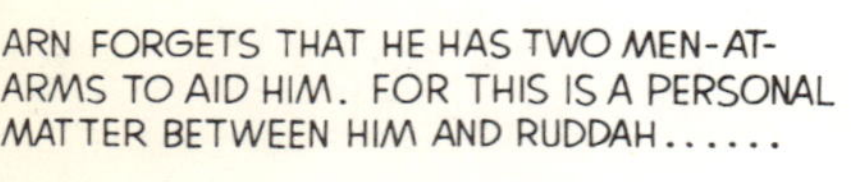

ARN FORGETS THAT HE HAS TWO MEN-AT-ARMS TO AID HIM. FOR THIS IS A PERSONAL MATTER BETWEEN HIM AND RUDDAH......

.....AND RUDDAH REACHES THE BOAT FIRST. *"LAUNCH YOUR BOAT, CHURL,"* HE COMMANDS, *"AND TAKE ME ACROSS THE RIVER, QUICKLY!"*

NEXT WEEK-**Against the Tide**

HAL FOSTER

1372

5-26-63